Christening Cakes

Christening Cakes

CYNTHIA VENN

MEREHURST

LONDON

Important: use only one set of measurements. The quantities given in metric are not always exact conversions of the imperial measurements. Cup conversions of imperial measurements are given below.

Imperial	Cups
5 fl oz liquid	⅔ cup
10 fl oz liquid	1¼ cups
20 fl oz liquid	2½ cups
40 fl oz liquid	5 cups
1lb granulated or caster (superfine) sugar	2 cups
1lb brown sugar	2 cups
1lb icing (confectioner's) sugar	3½ cups
1lb butter	2 cups
1lb flour	4 cups
1lb dried fruit	3 cups
8oz glacé cherries	1 cup
4oz chopped nuts	1 cup
4oz cocoa powder	1 cup
1oz flour	¼ cup
1oz granulated or caster (superfine) sugar	2 tablespoons
1oz butter	2 tablespoons

This book is dedicated to my husband Rob, who has given me so much encouragement. His assistance as critic, designer and morale-booster has helped to make this a very pleasurable task. Thanks to Katherine, Jonathan and Matthew for their patient acceptance of late dinners and sub-standard laundry service.
To Pat for her loyal friendship and support.

Published 1988 by Merehurst Ltd.
Ferry House, 51-57 Lacy Road, Putney, London SW15 1PR.

A catalogue record for this book is available from the British Library.

ISBN 1-85391-315-4 (paperback).

Managing Editor: Alison Leach.
Designer: Dave Copsey.
Cover Design by: Peter Bridgewater.
Photography by: Graham Tann, assisted by Lucy Baker.
Typeset by Ardek Photosetters.
Colour Separation by: Fotographics Ltd, London – Hong Kong.
Printed in Singapore by C. S. Graphics.

The Publishers wish to thank the following for their help and advice:

Edward Bunting and family.

The Covent Garden General Stores, 111 Long Acre, Covent Garden, London WC2.

Gold, silver and glass Christening gifts are available from a delightful selection at any of H Samuel's 400 branches nationwide.

Christening gifts from a selection at The White House, 51-52 New Bond Street, London W1. Tel. no: 071-629 3521.

House of Cakes, 18 Meadow Road, Stockport, Cheshire, for their excellent service in providing top quality cake dummies.

□ CONTENTS □

☐ FOREWORD ☐

It's not easy to design a cake for a new-born child who has not yet expressed a preference for teddy bears, bunnies or pussy cats, and the prospect of icing yet another stork is enough to drive you up the wall!

So I was delighted to see Cynthia Venn's charming selection of the prettiest, daintiest christening cakes ever. Her work is sheer perfection (so much so that she won first prize in the Masterclass section at the London branch of the British Sugarcraft Guild Christmas exhibition in 1986, and Cake of the Show two years earlier; also Cake of the Show at the 1986 Southdown exhibition).

Having been a cookery teacher for twelve years and subsequently run her own catering business, I not only admire her for finding the time to write this book, but also for her precise, practical instructions which I'm sure will help you to make christening cakes, that both you and the babies' parents will be proud of.

Mitzie Wilson
Cookery Editor
Best Magazine

□ *INTRODUCTION* □

A christening is one of the most important reasons for a family reunion and it is traditional to bake a very special cake in honour of the occasion. If a photograph is taken and kept in the family album, the child will later enjoy looking at his or her christening cake.

The cakes shown in this book range from the quick and simple designs to those involving more difficult techniques. I have tried to include a variety of styles to appeal to differing tastes and to many levels of skill.

The techniques used are explained in detail in a special section of the book. Smocking, which I developed for the International School of Sugar-craft, is illustrated here for the first time as an important feature of a cake.

Many of the designs can easily be adapted by removing the symbol of the christening and substituting flowers or other motifs appropriate to the occasion.

Cynthia Venn

□ CAKE RECIPES □

Rich Fruit Cake

These quantities make a 20-cm (8-in) round cake. For other sizes, the ingredients should be increased or decreased in the same proportions.

450g (1lb) sultanas
350g (12oz) raisins
225g (8oz) currants
65g (2½oz) nibbed almonds
65g (2½oz) citrus peel, chopped
100g (3½oz) glacé cherries
grated rind and juice of 1 lemon
45ml (3 tbsp) brandy
250g (9oz) butter or margarine
250g (9oz) soft brown sugar
4 eggs (at room temperature)
250g (9oz) plain (all-purpose) flour
2.5ml (½ tsp) mixed spice

Put the washed fruit, nuts, peel and cherries into a large mixing bowl with the lemon rind and juice. Moisten with the brandy, cover and leave to soak for several hours or overnight.

Grease a 20-cm (8-in) round cake tin (pan) and line with greaseproof paper.

Heat the oven to 150°C (300°F) Gas Mark 2.

Cream the butter and sugar until light and fluffy. Beat the eggs and add to the butter mixture a little at a time, beating thoroughly between each addition. If the mixture has a tendency to curdle, add a spoonful of the flour at this stage.

Sift the flour and spice together and add to the butter mixture, stirring thoroughly to combine smoothly. Turn into the prepared tin and level off the top.

Bake for about 3½–3¾ hours. To check if the cake is cooked, insert a clean skewer into the centre. If it comes out clean, the cake is cooked. Another test is to check that the mixture has stopped sizzling; it becomes quiet when it is cooked. Leave in the tin until the cake is quite cold.

Madeira Cake

This is a suitable recipe to use as an alternative to a rich fruit cake as it is firm enough to make a good base for decorating. To avoid the mixture curdling, all the ingredients should be at room temperature.

These quantities make a 20-cm (8-in) round or a 17.5-cm (7-in) square cake. For other sizes, the ingredients should be increased or decreased in the same proportions.

175g (6oz) butter
175g (6oz) caster (superfine) sugar
3 eggs, beaten
125g (4oz) self-raising flour
50g (2oz) plain (all-purpose) flour
50g (2oz) ground almonds
grated rind of 1 orange
about 30ml (2 tbsp) orange juice

Heat the oven to 175°C (350°F) Gas Mark 4.

Grease a 20-cm (8-in) round or a 17.5-cm (7-in) square cake tin (pan) and line with greaseproof paper.

Cream the butter and sugar until light and fluffy. Add the beaten eggs a little at a time, beating thoroughly between each addition.

Sift the flours and ground almonds together. Fold into the creamed mixture with the orange rind and enough orange juice to make a soft, dropping consistency. Turn the mixture into the prepared tin and bake for 1–1¼ hours. To check if the cake is cooked, insert a clean skewer into the centre. If it comes out clean, the cake is cooked. Leave in the tin for a few minutes, then turn out on to a wire cooling rack.

☐ ICING RECIPES ☐

Buttercream (basic)

This basic mixture can be coloured or flavoured as required.

125g (4oz) butter
175–225g (6–8oz) icing (confectioner's) sugar,
  sifted
few drops vanilla essence
15–30ml (1–2 tbsp) milk or evaporated milk

Cream the butter until soft. Beat in the sugar a little at a time, adding a few drops of vanilla essence and sufficient milk to give a fairly firm but spreading consistency.

Buttercream (rich)

The addition of an egg yolk makes this richer than the basic buttercream.

90g (3oz) butter
1 egg yolk
225g (8oz) icing (confectioner's) sugar, sifted
15ml (1 tbsp) orange or lemon juice or black coffee

Melt the butter in a saucepan or in a microwave.

Beat in the egg yolk. Gradually beat in the sugar and the chosen flavouring until the mixture is light and fluffy.

Flower Modelling Paste

Use this mixture when the weather is humid or if you wish the flowers to remain in good condition for a long time.

450g (1lb) icing (confectioner's) sugar
10ml (2 tsp) cornflour (cornstarch)
15ml (1 tbsp) gum tragacanth
10ml (2 tsp) powdered gelatine
25ml (5 tsp) cold water
10ml (2 tsp) white vegetable fat
10ml (2 tsp) liquid glucose
1 egg white, size 2 (large)

Sift the sugar, cornflour (cornstarch) and gum tragacanth into an ovenproof bowl. Heat gently in the oven or over a pan of boiling water until the sugar feels warm.

Sprinkle the gelatine on to the water and stand until the gelatine has absorbed all the water. Then dissolve over hot water or in a microwave. Do not allow the mixture to boil as this would destroy the elasticity. Remove from the heat and add the fat and liquid glucose.

Pour the liquids and the egg white into a well in the centre of the sugar mixture. Mix in a heavy-duty electric mixer on the slowest speed until the sugar has been incorporated. Increase the speed to maximum and mix until the paste is white and stringy. This will take about 5–10 minutes.

Put the paste into a strong polythene bag and keep this in a lidded container in the refrigerator overnight.

As this paste dries out very quickly, it must be kept covered. To use, cut off only the small quantity required and store the remaining paste in the refrigerator.

Flower Modelling Paste (easy)

Sugarpaste is obtainable from specialist cake decorating suppliers.

white vegetable fat
5ml (1 tsp) gum tragacanth
225g (8oz) commercial sugarpaste

Grease your hands with a little white fat and then knead the gum tragacanth into the sugarpaste. Store in an air-tight container and leave to rest overnight before using. It is not necessary to refrigerate this paste.

Gum Arabic Glaze

This glaze can be painted on any surface which requires a shine. It also makes a good adhesive. Rose water can be used instead of water but it is more expensive!

5ml (1 tsp) gum arabic (acacia) powder
15ml (1 tbsp) water

Add the gum arabic to the water and heat in a small bowl over hot water.

Heating the gum arabic will make it keep better.

Marzipan

125g (4oz) icing (confectioner's) sugar, sifted
125g (4oz) caster (superfine) sugar
225g (8oz) ground almonds
5ml (1 tsp) lemon juice
almond or vanilla essence
1 egg or 2 egg yolks, beaten

Mix together the sugars and the ground almonds. Make a well in the centre and add the lemon juice, a drop of the chosen essence and sufficient beaten egg to make a firm but malleable dough. Turn on to a work surface lightly dusted with icing (confectioner's) sugar and knead until firm. Do not over-knead as this will release too much oil from the almonds.

Wrap in plastic wrap or foil until required.

Modelling Paste

20ml (4 tsp) powdered gelatine
60ml (4 tbsp) water
10ml (2 tsp) liquid glucose
450g (1lb) icing (confectioner's) sugar, sifted

Soak the gelatine in the water until the water has been absorbed. Then dissolve over hot water until it becomes a clear liquid without any undissolved crystals. Do not allow the mixture to boil.

Remove from the heat and add the liquid glucose. Pour over the sugar and stir with a knife. Knead the mixture quickly on a board dusted with icing sugar until smooth.

Store at room temperature in an air-tight container.

Royal Icing

All the royal-iced cakes shown in this book were covered with this icing, made with pure albumen powder.

15g (½oz) pure albumen powder
90ml (3 fl oz) cold water
450g (1lb) icing (confectioner's) sugar, sifted

Stir the albumen powder into the water and leave to stand for up to 30 minutes. At first the mixture will appear lumpy but the powder will gradually dissolve. Stir thoroughly and pour through a sieve into the icing (confectioner's) sugar. Either mix by hand or with an electric mixer on the lowest speed for about 10 minutes until the icing stands in stiff peaks.

Icing made with an electric mixer must stand for 24 hours. Before using, stir vigorously with a wooden spoon to disperse the air bubbles.

For soft cutting, glycerine may be added to the finished icing in the proportion of 5ml (1 tsp) to 450g (1lb) sugar.

Royal Icing (for extension work)

Always use egg white in preference to albumen powder when making royal icing for extension, lace or filigree work, as this makes a stronger icing.

1 egg white
200–225g (7–8oz) icing (confectioner's) sugar, finely sifted
pinch gum arabic
1ml (¼ tsp) liquid glucose

Put the egg white in a ceramic or glass bowl, completely free from any grease. Take care that no egg yolk spills into the egg white.

Add the icing (confectioner's) sugar a teaspoon at a time, mixing well by hand. Continue adding sugar and beating until the icing reaches a soft peak stage. Then add the gum arabic and continue mixing. Finally add the liquid glucose and mix in well.

Keep the icing covered. It can be used immediately and is best when freshly made.

Sugarpaste

Sugarpaste, also known as fondant, has been used to cover several of the cakes shown in this book.

60ml (4 tbsp) cold water
15ml (1 tbsp) powdered gelatine
45ml (3 tbsp) liquid glucose
15ml (1 tbsp) glycerine
1kg (2lb) icing (confectioner's) sugar, sifted

Put the water in a basin and sprinkle the gelatine on top. Leave to soak until the gelatine has absorbed the water, about 30 minutes. Then place the basin in a saucepan containing about 2.5-cm (1-in) of boiling water and allow the gelatine to dissolve. This mixture should be clear and contain no crystals. Do not allow it to boil.

Remove from the heat and add the liquid glucose and glycerine. Stir until combined and leave to become cool, not cold.

Put half the sugar in a basin and make a well in the centre. Add the liquid ingredients and stir until the sugar has been absorbed. Transfer the mixture to an air-tight container and leave for 24 hours.

Knead the remaining sugar into the mixture until it is smooth and not sticky. Transfer to the air-tight container and rest for at least 1 hour before using.

□ SPECIAL TECHNIQUES □

Bas Relief

Bas relief is a form of three-dimensional modelling in which less than half of the true depth of the figure projects from the background. Sugarpaste should be used in preference to modelling paste as it remains soft, thus giving a longer period in which to work.

Transfer the design to the cake or plaque. The background, if any, should be completed by painting or brush embroidery before the bas relief is started.

Roll the sugarpaste out to about 6-mm (¼-in) thickness, or even thinner if the figure is to be very small.

Use a sharp knife to cut out the figure. Moisten the underneath of the figure and stick to the cake within the outline already marked. Generally, the contours of a figure can be defined quite well by depressing the low-lying areas or those appearing behind, but if you wish to emphasize an even more raised area, a small piece of sugarpaste may be tucked underneath before the figure is stuck down. Then commence the modelling. If necessary, decoration can be applied to the modelled figure by piping or by using the appliqué method.

As flower modelling paste can be rolled out thinner than sugarpaste, use this to clothe figures. The underclothes, such as a frilled petticoat, should be applied first, followed by the dress bodice and then the sleeve. The pieces should be cut out a little larger than the pattern as allowances must be made for the garment to cover the contours of the body and to be tucked underneath to give the impression that it continues around the back of the figure.

Briar Rose

1 Using flower modelling paste, make a golf tee shape. Roll out the flat part with the handle of a paintbrush and cut out the calyx.
2 Push a hooked wire through the calyx. Snip and thin the sepals. Curve and leave until semi-dry; this will help to support the petals.
3 Cut five petals with a rose petal cutter. Snip out a V-shape from the rounded edge.
4 Flute the edge and cup using a ball modelling tool. Leave the petals to stiffen for a few minutes over a domed shape such as a small ball or the back of a teaspoon.
5 Set the petals into the calyx with the points to the centre. Stick with egg white. Overlap each petal and space evenly. The last petal should have one edge tucked under the first petal.

6 Make a centre by pressing a small ball of the paste into a piece of net or wire mesh to make the appropriate markings. Stick into the centre of the flower with a little pale green icing. Stick very fine stamens around the centre into the trace of icing which is squeezed out from under the centre. Dust the edges of the petals with blossom tint.

Broderie Anglaise

1 Lay the template on the cake.
2 Prick out the pattern carefully with a scriber or headed pin.
3 Push holes into the sugarpaste with the handle of a paintbrush or knitting needle. Hold the brush or needle at an angle of 45° to make an oval shape for the petals.
4 Outline the holes with icing using a No0 nozzle. Pipe embroidery in between.

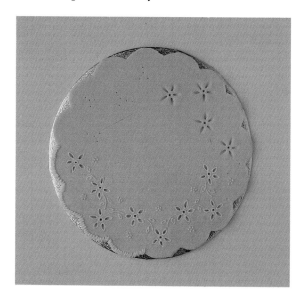

Brush Embroidery

This technique enables the decorator to produce effective designs quite simply and quickly. Brush embroidery looks equally good in colour on a white background or in white on a coloured background.

The effect is achieved by outlining the pattern, which has previously been transferred to the cake surface, with icing, using a No1 or No0 nozzle.

An inner line is piped and the petal or leaf is brushed from the outer edge down to the base, with a damp paintbrush. Work on the background first, completing one small area at a time, and gradually working to the foreground. The icing should be thickest at the edges, fading to just a wash at the base.

Use long, even strokes to avoid ridges and always brush leaves and petals in the direction which would be taken by the natural veining.

Top left: Outline of design scribed on to plaque
Top right: Background leaves completed first
Bottom left: Overlapping leaves and back petals of the flower
Bottom right: Front of the flower completed and stamens added

Extension Work

Simple extension work is generally used around the base of a cake. It consists of a bridge formed by piping a series of dropped loops with subsequent rows piped exactly on top of the previous row until it is about 6-mm (¼-in) deep. This bridge supports fine vertical lines which are piped from a straight or shaped line that has been previously marked on the side of the cake. A No0 or No00 nozzle is generally used.

Make a template the depth of the cake and the circumference of a round cake. For a square or hexagonal cake, a template of one side is sufficient.

Fold the template several times until you have folds about 2.5-cm (1-in) wide. Cut the

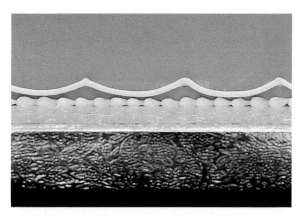

One row of dropped loops piped for the bridgework with a No1 nozzle

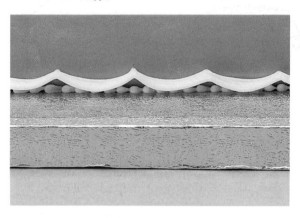

Six rows of bridgework completed — each row is left to dry before the next row is piped

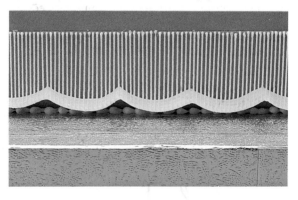

Straight extension work: threads of curtain work dropped from a guideline to the bridge and tucked underneath

template on one edge to the shape required for the top of the extension work. Fit around the cake and secure with masking tape. Mark a line for the top with a pin or scriber and also prick around the base on each fold line.

Some hints for successful extension work:
1 Make the icing with egg white as this will make stronger threads than albumen powder (see page 10).
2 Sift the sugar through a nylon stocking several times; this will help to prevent the nozzle blocking.

3   Tilt the cake towards you when piping curtain work to prevent the threads sagging towards the cake.

4   Use freshly made icing, preferably not made in an electric mixer.

5   Work with the cake at eye level.

6   Broken threads may be caused by the icing being too soft, by relaxing the pressure, by an air bubble or by using old icing.

7   The downward threads of extension work should be piped very close together so that another thread could not be piped in between.

Figure Piping

Figures may be either piped directly on to the cake or on to waxed paper or plastic wrap and transferred to the cake when dry. If using the second method for figures to be placed on the side of a round cake, the wet figure on waxed paper should be laid over the side of the tin (pan) in which the cake was baked so that, when dry, it will lie smoothly on the curved side of the cake.

The icing should be only slightly softer than that used for normal piping.

Half-fill a number of small vegetable parchment piping bags with the different coloured icing you require for the figure. Snip a small hole in the end of the bags.

It is not necessary to outline the sections. Simply fill each one with the appropriate coloured icing, starting with the areas which lie behind and finishing with the parts such as a plump cheek or puffed sleeve which are prominent. The latter should be generously filled to stand out from the rest of the figure.

It should be possible to pipe a figure with many different colours without waiting for each section to dry.

When dry, paint in the features, shading and details with a fine brush and food colouring.

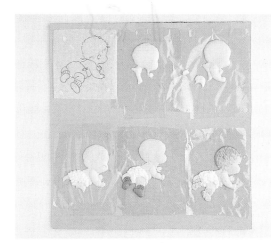

Flooded Collars

The icing used for collar work must not contain any glycerine. It should not be too old as the icing relaxes too much and looks rather wet; the run-out pieces are also very slow to dry. The appearance will not be as glossy as that of collars made with fresh icing.

Icing made in an electric mixer should be allowed to stand for at least 24 hours and then stirred vigorously with a wooden spoon to disperse the air bubbles before using.

Some food colourings, particularly paste ones, contain some glycerine. These should be used with caution as the glycerine will make the icing remain soft.

Place waxed paper or plastic wrap over the pattern, smooth it out carefully and secure with icing or masking tape, ensuring that there are no creases.

Outline the collar with a No1 nozzle, then flood the centre with softer icing. Add a little more albumen dissolved in water, or egg white, to icing of normal piping consistency to make run-out pieces stronger. The icing should be soft enough to settle down and produce a smooth, fine run-out. If it is too runny, it will flow over the side of the outline. If it is too thick, it will produce an uneven surface.

Half-fill a vegetable parchment piping bag with the soft icing and snip a small hole in the end. Do not use a nozzle for flood-work.

Fill the outline generously with the softened icing to make substantial run-out pieces with slightly domed surfaces. Use a paintbrush to coax the icing into any awkward little corners. Break any bubbles with the brush as soon as they appear on the surface.

To obtain a good sheen on collars and plaques, dry as quickly as possible near a gentle heat such as a radiator or under a lamp. Store on waxed paper until required.

When flooding a large collar to go all round a cake, first flood a small area, then go back to the beginning and add some icing to the other side. Continue in this way until the collar is complete. This will avoid there being an unsightly mark where the soft icing meets that which has already dried.

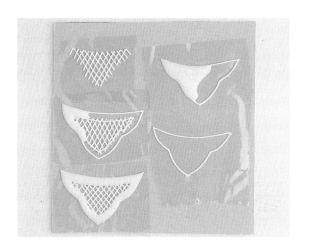

Ribbon Inserts

Cut evenly spaced pairs of slits in the sugarpaste. Cut lengths of ribbon about 12-mm (½-in) long. Push each end into a slot. Pipe embroidery to fill in and to disguise the cuts.

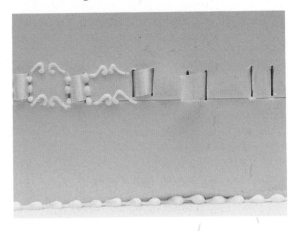

Frill cut into shape; one side cut and opened out; bottom edge frilled by rolling a cocktail stick (wooden toothpick) along the edge

Flounces and Frills

The sugarpaste used for covering the cake is generally used for making flounces and frills. It is not necessary to add anything such as gum tragacanth to the paste. The fullness is achieved by working on thinly rolled paste and stretching the lower edge by gently rolling a cocktail stick (wooden toothpick) across the edge until it is very thin and full.

The following points are important:
1   Roll out the sugarpaste on a work surface lightly dusted with icing (confectioner's) sugar.
2   Roll out the paste quite thinly; this will help to prevent the flounce or frill cracking.
3   Work as quickly as possible with freshly rolled sugarpaste.
4   Store flounces and frills in a dry place. Humidity will encourage them to droop. Sagging will also be caused by the flounces and frills being too thick and heavy.

Roll out the sugarpaste to about 3-mm (⅛-in) thickness. Cut out a fluted circle with a small, inner plain circle. A special frill cutter or a tartlet cutter can be used. Cut the inner hole with a plain circular cutter. The depth of the flounce or frill will be governed by the size of the central hole – a small centre will result in a wide flounce or frill.

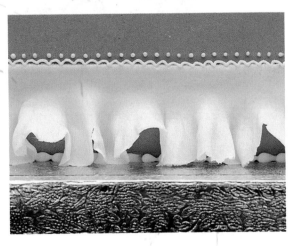

Flounce attached to cake

14

abcdefghijklmn
opqrstuvwxyz
ABCDEFGHIJ
KLMNOPQR
STUVWXYZ

AABCDEEFG
HIJKLMNOPQ
RSTUVWXYZ

□ *TOM* □

Ingredients

*fruit cake baked in 20-cm (8-in) square cake tin
  (pan)*
boiled, sieved apricot jam
700g (1½lb) marzipan
sherry or other alcohol
700g (1½lb) sugarpaste
black paste food colouring
burgundy paste food colouring
cornflower blue food colouring
flower modelling paste
royal icing

Equipment

27.5-cm (11-in) square cake board
pastry brush
rolling pin
sharp knife or scalpel
tracing paper
waxed paper or plastic wrap
vegetable parchment piping bags
No1 nozzle
tilting turntable or small wooden blocks
fine sable paintbrush
white cotton thread
blossom plunger cutter
scriber or headed pin

The baby giraffe is landing on the top of the cake by parachute to the surprise of its mother – a decoration to make the guests at the christening party smile!

Cover the cake with marzipan and pale blue-coloured sugarpaste in the usual way. Place the cake on the board.

Make a template of the parachute. Roll out a little modelling paste, lay the template on top and cut round the outline with a sharp knife or scalpel. Drape the parachute over a small orange or similarly shaped object, so that it will dry in a convex shape.

Make a template of the baby giraffe. Lay the template on a rigid board and cover with waxed paper or plastic wrap, carefully smoothing out any wrinkles. Using a No1 nozzle and white royal icing, pipe round the outline. Flood the inner area (see page 13) and leave to dry.

Make a template of the mother giraffe and run-out the figure in the same way. While the icing is still wet, drape the figure over the side of the cake and leave to dry on the waxed paper. To prevent the icing from sliding to one side, place the cake board on a tilting turntable or use blocks to wedge the board at a sharp angle. Alternatively, the mother giraffe could be draped over any other

exactly similar shape to dry. Dry in a warm place to achieve a good sheen.

Paint lines on the parachute and the features on the baby giraffe with food colouring. Place the parachute in position, attaching it to the top of the cake with a line of royal icing. Attach short strands of thread to the parachute with dots of royal icing, gather the ends together and stick to the cake. Place the baby giraffe so as to cover the ends of the thread.

Paint the features on the mother giraffe and stick in place over the side of the cake.

Using a template made from the basic lettering (see page 15), add the baby's name.

Decorate the cake with a few flowers made with a blossom plunger cutter.

Make a template of the rabbits and mark the outlines with a scriber or headed pin on the sides of the cake. Figure pipe (see page 13) directly on to the cake. Paint the rabbits with food colouring.

Finally pipe a snail's trail around the base of the cake.

Template for baby giraffe

Template for parachute

Template for large giraffe

Template for rabbits

18

☐ *BEN* ☐

Ingredients

fruit cake baked in 20-cm (8-in) round cake tin (pan)
boiled, sieved apricot jam
700g (1½lb) marzipan
sherry or other alcohol
700g (1½lb) royal icing
blue liquid food colouring
royal icing

Equipment

27.5-cm (11-in) round cake board
pastry brush
rolling pin
tracing paper
waxed paper or plastic wrap
vegetable parchment piping bags
No1 nozzle
No2 nozzle
No42 scroll nozzle
fine sable paintbrush
scriber or headed pin
tilting turntable or small wooden blocks
75-cm (¾-yard) white satin ribbon, 3-mm (⅛-in) wide

The initial impact of this cake is one of restrained formality, but look closely and enjoy the humour of the baby mouse asleep in a nut-shell and the frieze of storks flying around the sides.

Cover the cake with marzipan and place on the board. Then cover with blue-coloured royal icing and leave to dry. Coat the edge of the board with royal icing and leave to dry.

Make a template of the flying stork. Lay it on a rigid surface and cover with waxed paper or plastic wrap, carefully smoothing out any wrinkles. Fill a piping bag with white royal icing of medium peak consistency to define the feathers well. Cut a small hole in the end of the bag and use the figure piping technique (see page 13) for the stork. Make four birds. Leave to dry on the side of the tin in which the cake was baked to give a gentle curve so that the storks can easily be attached to the side of the cake.

Make a template for the brush embroidery and mark the outlines on the top of the cake with a scriber or headed pin. Complete the background following the brush embroidery technique (see page 12). Both the mouse baby and the cradle are figure piped

Tilt the cake and use dots of royal icing to attach the flying storks to the side, being careful to space them evenly.

Pipe a continuous chain of scrolls with a No42 scroll nozzle around the top edge of the cake. Overpipe with a No2 nozzle and then with a No1 nozzle.

Using a No1 nozzle, pipe a bead border around the base of the cake. Attach white ribbon around the cake just above the beading.

Using a template made from the basic lettering (see page 15), add the baby's name.

Template for flying stork

Template for mouse baby

☐ *OLIVIA* ☐

Ingredients

fruit cake baked in 20-cm (8-in) round cake tin
   (pan)
boiled, sieved apricot jam
700g (1½lb) marzipan
sherry or other alcohol
700g (1½lb) sugarpaste
flower modelling paste
royal icing
icing (confectioner's) sugar
cornflour (cornstarch)
twinkle pink blossom tint
briar roses and buds (see page 11)
modelled baby

Equipment

27.5-cm (11-in) round cake board
pastry brush
rolling pin
vegetable parchment piping bags
No0 nozzle
No1 nozzle
tracing paper
scalpel or sharp knife
cocktail stick (wooden toothpick)
wads of cotton wool
scriber or headed pin
ribbon insert cutter
1 metre (1 yard) pink satin ribbon, 3-mm (⅛-in)
   wide
knitting needle

A scalloped drape with broderie anglaise threaded with pink ribbon adds delicacy to this cake for a baby girl.

Cover the cake with marzipan and sugarpaste in the usual way. Using a No1 nozzle and royal icing, pipe a neat border around the base of the cake.

Mix some flower modelling paste with the same quantity of sugarpaste. It is possible to roll this mixture out very thinly and, when dry, it will hold the folds of the drape in position.

Make a circular template a little larger than the cake board. Fold firstly into quarters and continue to fold until you have thirty-two segments. Cut a scallop in the outer edge and unfold to form a pattern for the drape.

Roll out the paste very thinly. Lay the template on top and cut round the edge with a scalpel or sharp knife. Lay the drape on a work surface lightly dusted with cornflour (cornstarch) and frill the edge with a cocktail stick (see page 14).

Do not moisten the top of the cake before covering with the drape. Adjust the folds evenly.

If necessary, support the drape with wads of cotton wool until the folds are firm enough to hold their shape.

Mark a circle about 10-cm (4-in) in diameter with a scriber or headed pin in the centre of the top of the cake. Use a ribbon insert cutter to make slits and insert short lengths of pink satin ribbon around the circle.

Make a template of the broderie anglaise design. Lay this on the top of the cake and prick out the main outlines with a scriber or headed pin. Make holes for the petals by pressing a knitting needle into the paste at an angle of 45°. With a No0 nozzle, outline the holes and fill in with neat embroidery.

Using a template made from the basic lettering (see page 15), add the baby's name.

When the drape has set, dust the edge lightly with twinkle pink blossom tint.

Place a briar rose in the centre of the cake and tuck a modelled baby in the petals. Arrange briar roses and buds on the cake board.

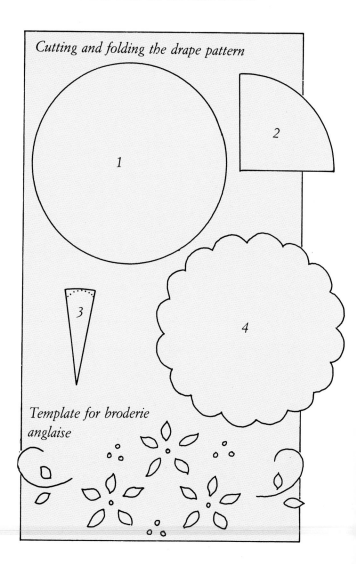

Cutting and folding the drape pattern

Template for broderie anglaise

☐ *ZOE* ☐

Ingredients
fruit cake baked in 15-cm (6-in) oval cake tin (pan)
boiled, sieved apricot jam
450g (1lb) marzipan
sherry or other alcohol
450g (1lb) sugarpaste
burgundy paste colouring
white royal icing
modelling paste

Equipment
25-cm (10-in) oval cake board
pastry brush
rolling pin
scalpel or sharp knife
vegetable parchment piping bags
No0 nozzle
No1 nozzle
No4 nozzle
waxed paper or plastic wrap
cocktail stick (wooden toothpick)
small plunger blossom cutter
medium carnation cutter
moulded flowers

This is a small cake with decoration to scale. If a larger cake were needed, the crib would have to be enlarged in proportion.

Cover the cake with marzipan and pale pink-coloured sugarpaste in the usual way. Place the cake on the board.

Using a No0 nozzle and white royal icing, pipe a delicate embroidered border on the top of the cake, about 12-mm (½-in) from the edge.

Place the crib on the top of the cake, securing it with dots of royal icing.

Model a small baby doll from flesh-coloured sugarpaste and place it in the crib. Roll out a piece of white modelling paste very thinly for the coverlet. Frill the edge slightly with a cocktail stick (wooden toothpick). Drape the coverlet over the edge of the crib, allowing it to hang in folds on one side. Decorate the crib with blossoms.

Measure the circumference of the cake and cut a strip of paper of the same length. Fold the paper into six sections and cut a deep scallop in the top edge. Unfold the paper and use to mark the guidelines with a scriber or headed pin for the positioning of the frilled sections on the side of the cake. The highest point of each scallop should be about half-way up the side of the cake.

To make the frilled sections, roll out some modelling paste very thinly. Use a medium carnation cutter to cut out each section. Frill the edges with a cocktail stick (wooden toothpick) and cut

holes with a No4 nozzle. Leave to dry, then use a No0 nozzle to pipe a fine decorative line above the frill.

Using a No1 nozzle and white royal icing, pipe a snail's trail around the base of the cake.

Attach the frilled sections to the side of the cake with tiny dots of royal icing, following the marked guidelines.

Stick the small blossoms in clusters around the side of the cake above the frilled sections.

Using a template made from the basic lettering (see page 15), add the baby's name.

The Crib
Roll out some modelling paste and cut out the shapes for the crib. Assemble and decorate with tiny, plunger-cut blossoms.

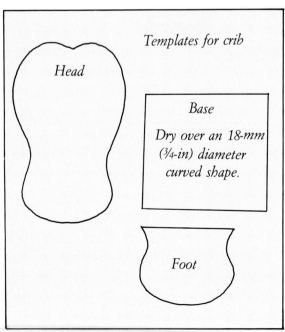

Templates for crib

Head

Base

Dry over an 18-mm (¾-in) diameter curved shape.

Foot

□ ANDREW □

Ingredients

fruit cake baked in 20-cm (8-in) round cake tin (pan)
boiled, sieved apricot jam
700g (1½lb) marzipan
sherry or other alcohol
700g (1½lb) royal icing
food colourings

Equipment

30-cm (12-in) round cake board
pastry brush
rolling pin
tracing paper
large board
waxed paper or plastic wrap
adhesive tape
vegetable parchment piping bags
No0 nozzle
No1 nozzle
No2 nozzle
fine sable paintbrush
scriber or headed pin
tilting turntable or small wooden blocks

A close look at the elaborate collar on this cake will reveal an intricate design of toys and animals.

Cover the cake with marzipan. Place on the board and cover with royal icing. Coat the edge of the board with royal icing. Leave to dry.

Make a template of the mouse design and, using a scriber or headed pin, prick out the design in three places on the side of the cake. Use the brush embroidery technique (see page 12) for the flowers and leaves, colouring these appropriately with food colourings.

The mice are flooded directly on to the cake, which should either be on a tilting turntable or wedged steeply with small blocks to prevent the icing slipping.

Make a template of the rosebud and mark the design on the top of the cake with a scriber. Complete with brush embroidery.

Using a template made from the basic lettering (see page 15), add the baby's name.

Make a template of the top collar and attach it to a large board. Cover with waxed paper or plastic wrap, carefully smoothing out any wrinkles and securing with adhesive tape or icing.

Using a No1 nozzle and royal icing, pipe the inner and outer lines of the collar. Flood (see page 13) the inside and outside borders with soft royal icing. Pipe the balls in royal icing with a No1 nozzle, making sure that there are no gaps between any of the connecting lines as this would weaken the collar. Pipe the bears with a No2 nozzle, both to emphasize and to add strength to the collar. Leave to dry.

Pipe tiny dots with a No0 nozzle around the outside of the collar to form a lacy edge. Leave in a dry place for at least 24 hours.

Using the template as a guide, pipe the outline of the collar in royal icing on the cake board with a No1 nozzle. Flood this collar with soft royal icing. Pipe a row of beads in royal icing with a No1 nozzle around the base of the cake. Use a No0 nozzle to pipe the lace edging to the board collar.

Using a No2 nozzle, pipe a ring of royal icing around the top edge of the cake. Carefully peel off the waxed paper or plastic wrap from the top collar and lift it on to the cake, lining the points up with those of the board collar. Finish by piping small dots of royal icing with a No1 nozzle around the inside of the collar.

Template for collar
NOTE: *Check diameter of finished cake before making collar to ensure it will fit.*

Template for rose

Template for mouse

□ *SIAN* □

Ingredients

fruit cake baked in 20-cm (8-in) round cake tin
  (pan)
boiled, sieved apricot jam
700g (1½lb) marzipan
sherry or other alcohol
700g (1½lb) sugarpaste
cream and other food colourings
royal icing

Equipment

27.5-cm (11-in) round cake board
pastry brush
rolling pin
tracing paper
scriber or headed pin
vegetable parchment piping bags
No0 nozzle
No1 nozzle
No2 nozzle
fine sable paintbrush
waxed paper or plastic wrap
Garrett circular frill cutter
cocktail stick (wooden toothpick)

A curved woodland frieze surrounds the sleeping baby. The naturalistic colouring is an unusual feature of this cake.

Cover the cake with marzipan and cream-coloured sugarpaste in the usual way. Place on the cake board.

Make a template of the picture and mark the position for the frame on the top of the cake with a scriber. Then prick out the outline of the baby. Complete the picture using the figure piping technique (see page 13) directly on to the cake, fading the icing out at the edges.

Place the design of the frame on a board and cover with waxed paper or plastic wrap, carefully smoothing out any wrinkles. Outline the frame with a No0 nozzle and cream-coloured royal icing. Flood each section of the picture with appropriately coloured icing, allowing each one to dry a little before flooding the adjacent area. When dry, outline the leaves with a darker shade of green. Use food colouring to brush shading on the rabbits and snail. Paint the baby's hair and features. Carefully remove the frame from the waxed paper or plastic wrap and stick in position

Template for rabbit

Template for framed picture

with a little icing.

With a No2 nozzle, pipe a snail's trail in royal icing around the base of the cake.

Measure the circumference of the cake and cut a strip of paper of the same length. Fold the paper into six and cut a scallop in the top. Unfold the paper and use as a guideline to mark the position for a single frill (see page 14). Drape the frill to form a shallow scallop. Pipe a scalloped line along the top of the frill.

Make a template for the rabbit. Figure pipe (see page 13) six rabbits on waxed paper or plastic wrap. Leave to dry and then paint with appropriate food colourings. Place a rabbit in each scallop, secure with a dot of royal icing and pipe blades of grass and flowers at each side of the rabbit.

Using a template made from the basic lettering (see page 15), add the baby's name.

☐ JENNY ☐

Ingredients

fruit cake baked in 20-cm (8-in) round cake tin (pan)
boiled, sieved apricot jam
700g (1½lb) marzipan
sherry or other alcohol
700g (1½lb) sugarpaste
Christmas red paste colouring
liquid food colourings
royal icing for extension work

Equipment

27.5-cm (11-in) round cake board
pastry brush
rolling pin
1 metre (1 yard) rose pink satin ribbon, 6-mm (¼-in) wide
1 metre (1 yard) rose pink satin ribbon, 1.5-mm (¹⁄₁₆-in) wide
scalpel or sharp knife
dogbone modelling tool
Dresden modelling tool
cocktail stick (wooden toothpick)
fine sable paintbrush
28-gauge white-covered wire
small blossom plunger cutter
piece of foam sponge
scriber or headed pin
vegetable parchment piping bags
No0 or No00 nozzle

The design of the little mouse watching over the cradle on this cake combines bas relief and brush embroidery.

Cover the cake with marzipan. Place the cake on the board and cover both with sugarpaste. Attach 6-mm (¼-in) wide ribbon around the cake board.

Because of the delicacy of the extension work, it is advisable to complete the modelling work on the top of the cake first.

Mark approximate guidelines on the surface of the cake for the moulded figures and the background blossoms. Complete the background first with brush embroidery (see page 12). Stick the bough in place with dots of royal icing. Place the mouse in position just touching the bough, and the cradle just below. Bend a little white-covered wire into shape and attach to the cradle and branch. Finish by sticking small cutter flowers at intervals along the wire.

Using a template made from the basic lettering (see page 15), add the baby's name.

Using a scriber or headed pin, mark a straight guideline about 3-cm (1¼-in) from the cake board. Then mark the scallops for the bridgework (see page 12).

Cut pieces of 1.5-mm (¹⁄₁₆-in) wide pink ribbon to fit the length between the guideline and the high points of the bridge. Attach with dots of royal icing at top and bottom. Follow instructions for curtain work (see page 12) and attach piped lace to the top edge.

Modelling the mouse and cradle

1 Cut out the shape of the mouse's head from sugarpaste and shape the snout by depressing the edges of the head and drawing it to a point at the centre. The ears are modelled from very small balls of paste.

2 Make the unclothed body of the mouse from a rough shape without an arm.

3 To clothe, roll out some modelling paste very thinly and cut a piece large enough to cover the body and tuck underneath. Stick clothes to the body with egg white and adjust the folds. Cut out a piece of white sugarpaste for the apron, frill the edge and stick in position. The mob cap is made with a small mound of paste. Stick in place between the ears and attach a narrow frill.

4 Model the shape of the arm, cover with a sleeve and attach to the body.

5 Make a feeding bottle and put it in the paw.

6 Model a piece of light brown-coloured paste into the shape of a walnut shell and leave to dry.

7 Model a canopy by hollowing a ball of paste and stick inside the shell. Leave to dry. Attach a frill.

8 Make a bough from small blossoms and leaves wired together.

Template for design on
top of the cake

☐ JAMES ☐

Ingredients

fruit cake baked in 20-cm (8-in) square cake tin (pan)
boiled, sieved apricot jam
700g (1½lb) royal icing
orange food colouring
yellow food colouring

Equipment

30-cm (12-in) square cake board
pastry brush
rolling pin
tracing paper
waxed paper or plastic wrap
vegetable parchment piping bags
No0 nozzle
No1 nozzle
No2 nozzle
fine sable paintbrush
2 metres (2¼ yards) yellow satin ribbon, 1.5-mm (¹⁄₁₆-in) wide
1.25 metres (1⅓ yards) yellow satin ribbon, 3-mm (⅛-in) wide
silver banding
moulded or piped flowers

The filigree work on the collars gives an unusual Spanish effect to this striking design, while the side panels are decorated with the traditional emblem of a stork.

Cover the cake with marzipan. Place on the board and cover with royal icing. Coat the edge of the board with royal icing. Leave to dry.

Make a template of the collar and place it on a rigid surface. Cover with waxed paper or plastic wrap, carefully smoothing out any wrinkles. Using a No0 nozzle, pipe the filigree work first and then using a No1 nozzle, pipe the outline, ensuring that it is attached to the filigree at all points. Flood the border at the inner and outer edges, also the central area of the collar where it thickens. Leave to dry. Pipe rows of dots around the outline to give a picot edge.

Four collars are needed for the top of the cake and four for the base. It may be wise to make a spare collar in case one is damaged accidentally. For the base collars, the inner edges can be quite narrow, piped with a No2 nozzle instead of flooding.

Carefully peel off the waxed paper or plastic wrap from the four base collars and place in position. Secure them by piping a line of beading around the base of the cake. Attach the 1.5-mm (¹⁄₁₆-in) wide ribbon around the cake above the beading.

Make a template of the plaque for the stork and place it on a rigid surface. Cover with waxed paper or plastic wrap, carefully smoothing out any wrinkles. Using a No1 nozzle and yellow-coloured royal icing, pipe around the outline and flood. Leave to dry. Four plaques are needed.

Make a template of the stork and place it on a rigid surface. Cover with waxed paper or plastic wrap, carefully smoothing out any wrinkles. Figure pipe (see page 13) the stork. Four are needed. Leave to dry. Using a fine sable paintbrush and the appropriate food colourings, paint the beak, legs and eye of each stork. Attach the storks to the plaques with dots of royal icing. Leave to dry and then position one in the centre of each side of the cake, securing with dots of royal icing.

To make the rattles, pipe large beads of royal icing on waxed paper or plastic wrap with a No1 nozzle. Add lines ending in small rings for the handles. Four are needed. Decorate with dots of royal icing to complement the chosen colour scheme.

Wrap silver banding around the edges of the cake board and cover with 3-mm (⅛-in) wide yellow satin ribbon.

Using a No1 nozzle, pipe a line of icing around the top edges of the cake, close to where the collars will be. Carefully peel off the waxed paper or plastic wrap from the collars and position one at each corner. Using a No2 nozzle, pipe a line around the top edges of the cake within the collars. Pipe a second line with a No1 nozzle on top of the first and also alongside it. Using yellow-coloured royal icing and No0 nozzle, overpipe all the lines.

Decorate the top of the cake with moulded or piped flowers. Place the rattles, crossed in pairs, in opposite corners.

Using a template made from the basic lettering (see page 15), add the baby's name. If preferred, the name may be piped directly on to the cake but this should be done before the top collars are attached.

Template for oval plaque

Template for stork

Template for collar

□ *KATHERINE* □

Ingredients

fruit cake baked in 20-cm (8-in) round cake tin (pan)
boiled, sieved apricot jam
700g (1½lb) marzipan
sherry or other alcohol
700g (1½lb) sugarpaste
about 225g (8oz) royal icing for extension work and brush embroidery
black food colouring
moss green food colouring
paprika food colouring
yellow food colouring

Equipment

27.5-cm (11-in) round cake board
pastry brush
rolling pin
tracing paper
scriber or headed pin
75-cm (¾-yard) white satin ribbon, 3-mm (⅛-in) wide
piece of perspex (plexiglas)
vegetable parchment piping bags
No00 nozzle
No0 nozzle
No1 nozzle
very small petal nozzle
fine sable paintbrush
waxed paper or plastic wrap
moulded flowers

The translucent effect of the baby's dress is achieved by using the brush embroidery technique (see page 12). By piping and brushing this in white on to a tinted base the shadows are accentuated.

Cover the cake with marzipan and sugarpaste tinted with green mixed with a speck of black. Cover the board with green-tinted sugarpaste and place the iced cake in position. Leave to harden for a few days.

Make a template of the guide for the extension work. Mark the scalloped outline with a scriber or headed pin on the side of the cake. Attach 3-mm (⅛-in) wide ribbon around the base of the cake, securing with a dot of royal icing.

Lay a piece of perspex (plexiglas) on top of the cake and invert, so that the cake board is on top.

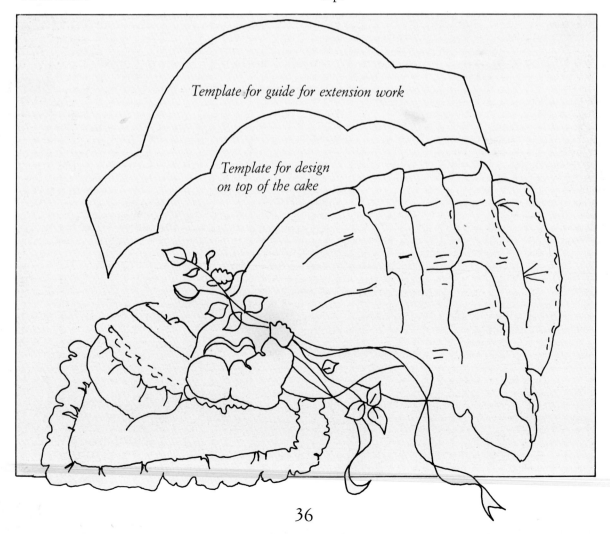

Template for guide for extension work

Template for design on top of the cake

Using a No1 nozzle, pipe the bridgework following the guidelines. Build up about six rows, allowing each one to dry before adding the next. Leave to dry thoroughly before inverting the cake to its original position.

The top decoration should be completed before undertaking the delicate extension work.

Make a template of the baby and lay it on the top of the cake to transfer the design, allowing the bottom of the hem to fall slightly over the edge. With a No0 nozzle and white royal icing, start with the pillow, following the sequence described for brush embroidery. After the pillow has been completed, start working upwards in layers from the hem of the dress. Then pipe and brush through the sleeve and hands. Pipe in trailing pink ribbons. Fill in the baby's face with fairly soft icing (see page 12). Pipe and brush in the bonnet, leaving the turned-back brim until last. Use a fine sable paintbrush and food colouring to paint in the baby's features. The rosebuds in the baby's hands are piped with a very small petal nozzle.

Using a template made from the basic lettering (see page 15), add the baby's name.

Pipe the extension work on the side of the cake with a No00 or No0 nozzle (see page 12).

With a No0 nozzle pipe fine lace pieces on waxed paper or plastic wrap. Leave to dry, then attach to the top edge of the extension work with dots of royal icing. Finish the bottom edge of the extension work with small loops or dots.

Arrange tiny posies of flowers around the base of the cake.

□ *PAUL* □

Ingredients

fruit cake baked in 20-cm (8-in) petal-shaped cake tin (pan)
boiled, sieved apricot jam
700g (1½lb) marzipan
sherry or other alcohol
700g (1½lb) sugarpaste
brown paste colouring
Christmas red, cornflower blue and lemon food colourings (for flowers)
moss green and black food colourings (for leaves)
paprika food colouring
flower modelling paste

Equipment

27.5-cm (11-in) round cake board
pastry brush
rolling pin
Dresden modelling tool
scriber or headed pin
knitting needle
waxed paper or plastic wrap

vegetable parchment piping bags
No0 nozzle
No1 nozzle
No2 nozzle
fine sable paintbrush
moulded flowers
white satin ribbon loops

The baby, modelled in bas relief, is framed by a circle of broderie anglaise and lace. The christening gown has tucked detail.

Cover the cake with marzipan in the usual way. Cover both the cake and board with sugarpaste. Place the cake on the board. Leave to dry.

Roll out some flesh-coloured sugarpaste about 6-mm (¼-in) thick. Cut out the shape of the baby's head. Shape with a Dresden modelling tool, pressing low areas and smoothing contours with your finger until you have a rounded head with plump cheeks, a tiny nose and a little chin. Smooth down the edges of a roughly shaped body and model into a rounded shape.

Template for design on top of the cake

The baby's gown is made from thinly rolled flower modelling paste. Cut out a roughly shaped bodice, a little larger than the body, to allow for tucking underneath it. Lay it on the body and stick with a little unbeaten egg white. Cut a skirt piece and gather into tucks to give fullness; attach to the bodice with a little egg white. Make an arm and a hand and cover with a sleeve in the same way. Attach to the baby and conceal the joins with piping. Paint in the hair and features. Make a pillow and add a frill to it. Finally roll out some modelling paste very thinly for the blanket and arrange in folds.

Mark a 15-cm (6-in) diameter circle on the cake with a scriber. Make a template of the top

design and use to prick out the pattern for the broderie anglaise and the outline for the centre-piece. Complete the broderie anglaise (see page 11). Pipe pieces of lace and leave to dry.

Position the baby in the frame. Attach the lace pieces around the frame, using dots of royal icing, and leave to dry.

Using a No2 nozzle, pipe a snail's trail border around the base of the cake.

Using a template made from the basic lettering (see page 15), add the baby's name.

Arrange a spray of moulded flowers on the top of the cake and tiny posies with ribbon loops in each indentation of the side of the cake at the base.

□ SIMON □

Ingredients

fruit cake baked in 20-cm (8-in) square cake tin (pan)
boiled, sieved apricot jam
700g (1½lb) marzipan
sherry or other alcohol
700g (1½lb) sugarpaste
burgundy paste colour
cornflower blue paste colour
flower modelling paste

Equipment

27.5-cm (11-in) square cake board
pastry brush
rolling pin
tracing paper
scriber or headed pin
27.5-cm (11-in) square of perspex (plexiglas) or glass
scalpel or sharp knife
palette knife
Dresden modelling tool
fine sable paintbrush
cocktail stick (wooden toothpick)
vegetable parchment piping bag
No0 nozzle
tilting turntable or 2.5-cm (1-in) high wooden blocks

Smocking has long been associated with baby clothes, so it makes a very appropriate, new technique for decorating a christening cake.

Cover the cake with marzipan and blue-coloured sugarpaste in the usual way. Place on the cake board.

Mark a guideline with a scriber around the cake 12-mm (½-in) from the base of the cake. Place the cake on a tilting turntable or use wedges to tilt the cake away from you. Make a gathered strip of smocking following the instructions and moisten a section of the cake above the line and about the width of the strip. Lift the gathered strip with a palette knife and keeping the gathers close together, attach the base of the strip to the guideline. Repeat the process until you have a continuous strip all round the cake, each section neatly butted up to the previous one.

Place a square of perspex (plexiglas) or glass on top and turn the cake upside down. Make a narrow frill (see page 14) and attach to the top edge with egg white. Leave to dry, then turn the cake back to its original position. The frill should now be turning towards the top of the cake. Make another frill and attach to the bottom of the smocking. Pipe embroidery stitches as shown.

Decorate the top of the cake with the knitting design, piping the baby's name in the trailing wool.

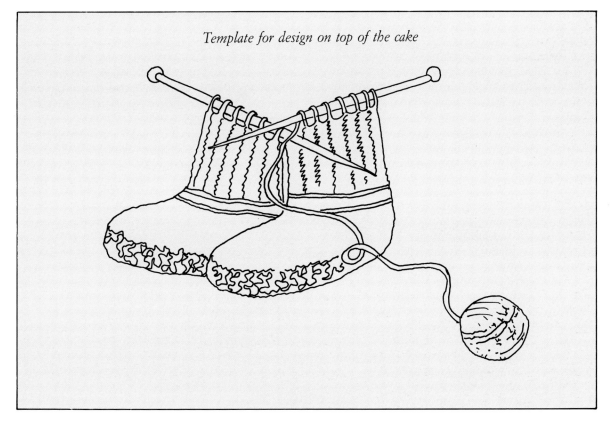

Template for design on top of the cake

Smocking

Use equal quantities of flower modelling paste and sugarpaste.

1 Cut a strip of thinly rolled paste 4-cm (1¼-in) wide. Make tucks with cocktail sticks (wooden toothpicks) as shown, repeating to the end of the strip.

2 Mark the honeycomb pattern by pressing the folds into shape while still soft. (If a different style of smocking is to be used, follow the chosen pattern.)

3 With a No0 nozzle pipe embroidery where marked in the honeycomb pattern.

4 Attach narrow frills at the top and bottom using egg white. Pipe a row of small 'stitches' to cover the joins.

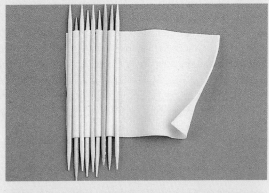
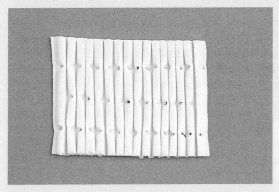
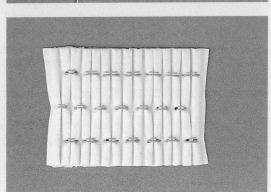
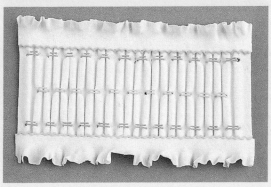

Booties

1 Roll out some sugarpaste about 6-mm (¼-in) thick. Lay the template on top and cut out the shape. Mark the same outline on the cake and attach the cut-out shape within that outline.

2 Smooth the edges with a Dresden modelling tool. Mark the toe of the top bootie by depressing the area immediately behind it. Mark the ribbing on the leg and holes for the ribbon.

3 Using a No0 nozzle, pipe the stitching. Insert narrow ribbon pieces. Make the knitting needles by rolling out thin sausage shapes of modelling paste. Point one end and attach a knob to the other. Leave to dry, then stick in position with icing.

The ball of wool is made from a small ball of paste covered with piped lines. Pipe stitches on the needles and leave a trail of wool incorporating the baby's name leading to the ball.

□ *MATTHEW* □

Ingredients

fruit cake baked in 20-cm (8-in) round cake tin (pan)
boiled, sieved apricot jam
700g (1½lb) marzipan
sherry or other alcohol
700g (1½lb) royal icing
royal icing (without glycerine) for filigree work
blue liquid food colouring
flesh-coloured modelling paste

Equipment

30-cm (12-in) round cake board
pastry brush
rolling pin
tracing paper
waxed paper or plastic wrap
vegetable parchment piping bags
No0 nozzle
No1 nozzle
No2 nozzle
scriber or headed pin
tilting turntable or 5-cm (2-in) wooden blocks
pieces of foam
fine sable paintbrush

A lattice-work cradle decorates the top of this cake with slanting filigree panels on the side.

Cover the cake with marzipan. Place on the board and coat the cake with blue-coloured royal icing. When dry, coat the board with royal icing. Leave to dry.

Make a template of the filigree panel. Place on a rigid surface and cover with waxed paper or plastic wrap, carefully smoothing out any wrinkles. Using a No0 nozzle, pipe the filigree, attaching each line firmly to another. Then pipe the outline around the filigree making sure that it is attached at all touching points. Pipe an outer line and flood the narrow border with soft royal icing (see page 13). Leave to dry.

Pipe dots of royal icing around the curved edge, leaving the straight edge plain. Leave to dry.

Twelve panels are used but it may be wise to make an extra one in case of accidental damage.

Make a template for the top of the cake and fold into twelve triangular sections. Unfold the paper and mark each section on the cake with a small dot. Make a corresponding dot on the base of the cake.

Using a No2 nozzle, pipe beading around

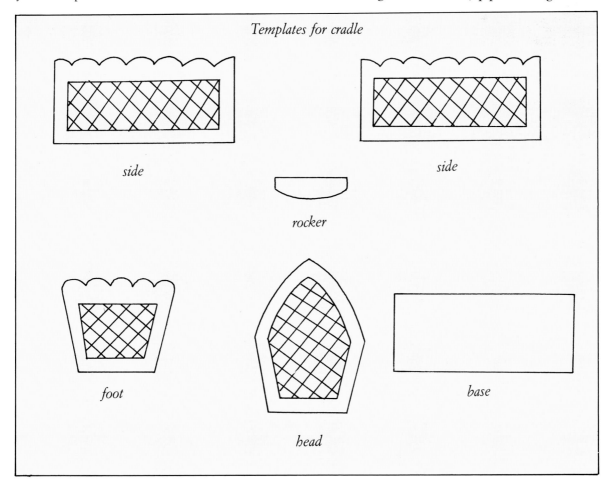

Templates for cradle

side   *side*

rocker

foot   *head*   *base*

Template for plaque

Template for filigree fin

the base of the cake, leaving small gaps where the filigree panels are to be attached.

Re-fold the template for the top of the cake and cut a scallop in the base of the triangle. Unfold the template and lay on top of the cake, lining up the points with the dots. Mark the line of the scallops on the cake with a scriber. Fill in the curved areas with cornelli work, using a No0 nozzle. Pipe an outline with a No2 nozzle. Overpipe with a No1 nozzle and pipe another line alongside.

Place the cake on a tilting turntable or use wedges under the board. With a No0 nozzle and tilting the cake away from you, pipe the decorations on the side of the cake.

Carefully peel off the waxed paper or plastic wrap from the filigree panels. Pipe a line of icing along the straight edge with a No1 nozzle. Attach to the side of the cake, lining up with the dots. Repeat with each filigree panel. They should all be attached at the same angle. Use pieces of foam to support them until they are dry. Then pipe a row of dots over each join.

Make a template of the plaque and cover with waxed paper or plastic wrap, carefully smoothing out any wrinkles. Using a No0 nozzle, pipe the outline and then flood the plaque (see page 13). Leave to dry. Pipe a fine bead border around the edge with a No0 nozzle. Leave to dry, then attach to the top of the cake with a dot of royal icing.

Make a template of the cradle components and cover with waxed paper or plastic wrap, carefully smoothing out any wrinkles. Pipe the lattice work first, using a No0 nozzle, then pipe the outlines. With soft royal icing in a piping bag

with a small hole cut in the end, fill in the border on each piece. The base of the cradle is solid. Leave to dry. Assemble the cradle as shown in the photograph, using cardboard supports to hold the pieces in position while drying. Lay a modelled baby in the cradle and cover with a blanket (see page 24).

Decorate the cradle and plaque with tiny blue flowerheads.

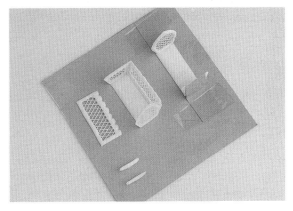

□ *JULIA* □

Ingredients

fruit cake baked in 20-cm (8-in) oval cake tin (pan)
boiled, sieved apricot jam
700g (1½lb) marzipan
sherry or other alcohol
700g (1½lb) sugarpaste
Christmas red paste colouring
royal icing
flower modelling paste
pink blossom tint

Equipment

27.5-cm (11-in) oval cake board
pastry brush
rolling pin
scalpel or sharp knife
tracing paper
scriber or headed pin
ribbon insert cutter
vegetable parchment piping bags
No0 nozzle
No1 nozzle
cocktail stick (wooden toothpick)
1 metre (1 yard) pink satin ribbon, 6-mm (¼-in)
  wide
2 metres (2¼ yards) pink satin ribbon, 3-mm
  (⅛-in) wide
50-cm (½-yard) pink satin ribbon, 1.5-mm (1/16-in)
  wide
green and white satin ribbon loops and trails,
  1.5-mm (1/16-in) wide
moulded sugar flowers
medium thick sable paintbrush

The delicate details of the design of this cake combine several of the techniques described on pages 11 – 14. Only very skilled cake decorators will be able to reproduce this cake.

Cover the cake with marzipan in the usual way. Roll out enough pink-coloured sugarpaste about 12-mm (½-in) thick to cover the top of the cake only. Moisten the top of the marzipanned cake with sherry or other alcohol. Lay the sugarpaste over the cake and trim the edges. Using a cutter or a template, cut out an oval shape through to the marzipan. Smooth the edges.

Roll out the remaining sugarpaste to the usual thickness and cover the whole cake in the usual way. Gently mould the sugarpaste around the oval hollow.

Make a template of the broderie anglaise design and prick out with a scriber on top of the cake. Complete as described on page 11.

Attach the 6-mm (¼-in) pink ribbon around the edge of the cake board.

To make the sleeping baby

1   Make the baby's head in a mould and cut in half lengthways. Alternatively, model using the bas relief technique (see page 11).
2   Make a rough body shape with white sugarpaste. Roll out a piece of flower modelling paste mixed with an equal quantity of sugarpaste. Cut out a rectangle and wrap around the figure like a cylinder.
3   Attach a frill to the bottom of the underskirt. Then add another row of frills.
4   Cut out another piece of thinly rolled paste the length of the figure and wide enough to cover and tuck underneath. The bottom edge should be wider than the top. Frill the bottom edge with a cocktail stick (wooden toothpick). Attach with egg white or gum arabic glue.
5   Cut a piece of thinly rolled paste to form the jacket, frill the edge and attach.
6   Shape a piece of paste for the arm and hand. Cover with a sleeve.
7   Mould a strip of paste around the head for a bonnet and attach a narrow frill.
8   When the pieces are dry, stick the head to the body with icing.
9   Make the shawl from a circle of thinly rolled paste and frill the edge. Arrange in folds and support with cotton wool or foam until it is dry.
10   Make a pillow and attach to the shawl.
11   When the baby is complete, lift on to the shawl.

Measure the circumference of the cake and cut a strip of paper of the same length. Fold it into eight sections and cut a scallop in the top edge. Using this as a guide, cut slits with a ribbon insert cutter and insert pieces of 3-mm (⅛-in) wide pink satin ribbon (see page 14).

Using a template made from the basic lettering (see page 15), add the baby's name to the side of the cake.

Combine equal quantities of white flower modelling paste and white sugarpaste and use to make fine, graduating frills (see page 14). Use a medium thick sable paintbrush to dust the frills with pink blossom tint. With a No0 nozzle pipe a small bead edging above the frills.

Lay the sleeping baby in the hollow in the top of the cake and frame with pieces of lace. Add a little spray of flowers and ribbon loops.

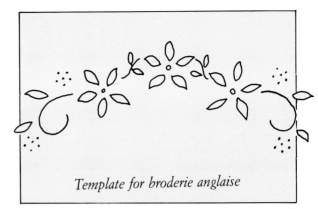

Template for broderie anglaise

☐ *JESSICA* ☐

Ingredients
fruit cake baked in 20-cm (8-in) round cake
*   *tin (pan)*
boiled, sieved apricot jam
700g (1½lb) marzipan
sherry or other alcohol
225g (8oz) modelling paste
cornflour (cornstarch)
pink food colouring

Equipment
27.5-cm (11-in) round cake board
pastry brush
rolling pin
tracing paper
waxed paper or plastic wrap
vegetable parchment piping bags
No1 nozzle
No2 nozzle
No44 rope nozzle
scriber or headed pin
piece of foam
wads of cotton wool
small plunger blossom cutter

This cake will appeal particularly to the more ambitious sugarcraft artist. The delicate 'cage' is an original idea for decorating the side of a cake.

Cover the cake with marzipan. Place on the board and cover the cake and the edge of the board with royal icing, giving the cake two coats of icing. (To achieve a soft cutting texture, 5ml (1 teasp) of glycerine can be added to 450g (1lb) of the icing.) Leave to dry.

Using a No2 nozzle, pipe a row of beading around the base of the cake.

Roll out the modelling paste to about 3-mm (⅛-in) thick on a work surface lightly dusted with cornflour (cornstarch). Make a template of the crescent and use to cut out 24 shapes. Leave to dry on a flat surface.

Cut out a 20-cm (8-in) diameter circle of tracing paper. Fold this in half, then in half again and repeat until you have 24 sections. Unfold the paper and lay it over the top of the cake. Using a scriber or headed pin, mark the position of each crease on the edge of the cake.

Using a No1 nozzle, pipe a line of icing on the straight edge of each crescent shape and stick to the side of the cake at the positions marked, taking care to keep each crescent at right angles.

Colour some of the icing with pink food colouring. With a No1 nozzle, pipe loops from one crescent to the next. It is easier to keep the lines neat and even by completing one section at

a time, working from top to bottom.

Using a plunger cutter, cut out about 250 small pink blossoms and shape each on a piece of foam. Attach with a dot of icing in lines down the edge of the crescent shapes. Pipe a dot of white icing in the centre of each blossom.

Re-fold the circle of tracing paper and cut the edge into a scalloped shape. Unfold the paper and lay it over the top of the cake. Outline the edge with a scriber or headed pin. Using a No44 rope nozzle and white icing, pipe a rope border following the outline. Overpipe with a No2 nozzle and pink-coloured icing. Then using a No1 nozzle and pink-coloured icing, pipe a line inside the rope border following the shape of the scallops.

Model a baby following the instructions on page 46 but leaving the head whole, so that it is shown full-face, with the baby lying on its back. Make a blanket from thinly rolled modelling paste. Drape this neatly and support the folds with wads of cotton wool until they are dry. Lay the dressed baby on the blanket and arrange on the cake with a cluster of small flowers beside it.

Pipe the baby's name in appropriately coloured icing, using run-out letters on waxed paper. Leave to dry before attaching to the cake with dots of icing.

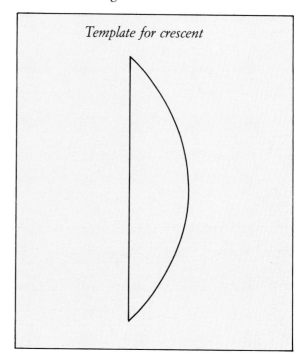

Template for crescent

☐ ANNA ☐

Ingredients

fruit cake baked in 20-cm (8-in) hexagonal cake tin (pan)
boiled, sieved apricot jam
700g (1½lb) marzipan
sherry or other alcohol
700g (1½lb) sugarpaste
black paste food colouring
claret paste food colouring
cornflower blue paste food colouring
modelling paste
royal icing
cornflour (cornstarch)

Equipment

27.5-cm (11-in) hexagonal cake board
pastry brush
rolling pin
tracing paper
scriber or headed pin
Garrett circular frill cutter
plain round cutter
cocktail stick (wooden toothpick)
vegetable parchment piping bags
No0 nozzle
No1 nozzle
2 metres (2¼ yards) pink satin ribbons, 1.5-mm (1/16-in) wide
1 metre (1 yard) pink satin ribbon, 12-mm (½-in) wide
moulded flowers

This hexagonal cake has a treble flounce at the corners, graduating to a single flounce in the centre of each side. The under-flounce is pink, shading through to pale lilac on top.

Cover the cake in the usual way with marzipan and sugarpaste, delicately tinted with claret mixed with blue and a touch of black paste colouring.

Measure round the sides of the cake and cut a piece of paper of the same length. Fold the paper in six sections and cut a shallow scallop in the top. Unfold the paper and use as a guideline to mark the flounce with a scriber, ensuring that the marks on the points of the cake are level.

Colour some sugarpaste pale pink and roll out very thinly. Cut out a fluted circle with a frill cutter and remove the centre with a plain round cutter, or use a frill cutter with centre attached. Cut the ring in half and frill the fluted edges as described on page 14 . Dampen the plain edge of the half circle and stick this piece to a point below the marked lines, evenly distributing the frill. Repeat with the other half circle.

Colour some more sugarpaste a deeper shade of pink and roll out as before. Cut each half circle in three and frill as before. Attach the shorter lengths above the first frill, covering the points and tapering off in between. The top layer is made by opening out the circle of paste on one side, frilling and arranging over the previous layers. Take care to position this flounce exactly on the guideline and to keep the corner points neat and sharp.

Pipe a neat line of beading at the top edge of the frill with a No0 nozzle. Attach tiny bows made from 1.5-mm (1/16-in) wide ribbon at each point above the flounce.

Embroider the design on the sides of the cake in white royal icing.

To make the bib, roll out the white modelling paste very thinly on a work surface lightly dusted with cornflour (cornstarch). Make a template, lay it on the modelling paste and cut out the bib. Arrange it in folds before the modelling paste sets and leave to dry. If the folds have a tendency to droop, they can be supported with icing nozzles or wads of cotton wool until they are dry. Pipe a neat edging and embroider the bib. Attach to the cake with dots of royal icing.

Using a template made from the basic lettering (see page 15), add the baby's name.

Finish the cake with an arrangement of ribbons and flowers.

Attach the 12-mm (½-in) pink satin ribbon to the edges of the cake board.

Template for bib

□ *JOHN* □

Ingredients
fruit cake baked in 20-cm (8-in) round cake tin (pan)
boiled, sieved apricot jam
700g (1½lb) marzipan
sherry or other alcohol
700g (1½lb) royal icing
blue liquid food colouring
royal icing for collars

Equipment
30-cm (12-in) round cake board
30-cm (12-in) thin round cake board
rolling pin
pastry brush
tracing paper
waxed paper or plastic wrap
vegetable parchment piping bags
No1 nozzle
No2 nozzle
tilting turntable or wooden blocks
scriber or headed pin
silver banding
large piece of foam
moulded flowers

The traditional theme of the stork carrying the baby is flooded on to the top of the cake, framed by filigree collars. This design requires a high degree of skill from the decorator.

Cover the cake with marzipan. Place on the board and coat with pale blue-coloured royal icing in the usual way. Coat the board with royal icing. Leave to dry.

Make a template of the filigree collar. Lay on a rigid surface and cover with waxed paper or plastic wrap, carefully smoothing out any wrinkles. Using medium peak royal icing and a No1 nozzle, pipe over all the outlines, taking care that all the lines of the filigree are securely attached to one another. Flood the collar where indicated and the stork and baby with soft royal icing. It is important that no area of the flood-

work is left too long so that the surface begins to dry (see page 13); otherwise there will be a mark where the soft icing joins an area which has been allowed to dry. This collar will necessitate quite a lot of moving from one place to another.

To make the board collar, make a plain template of the top collar, omitting the stork and baby. Cut out a central circle of sufficient diameter for the template to fit over the cake on to the board. Pipe an outline around the edge of the template with a No1 nozzle, using medium peak royal icing. Remove the template and flood the collar directly on to the board with soft icing. Leave to dry.

Using a No2 nozzle, pipe a row of neat beads around the base of the cake to conceal the join.

Outline the board collar with rows of line-work. Start with a No2 nozzle, then pipe a line with a No1 nozzle on top of the first line and another line alongside.

Attach silver banding to the edge of the cake board.

Make templates of the side line-work. Place the cake on a tilting turntable or use wedges. Tilt the cake at a sharp angle and lay the template against the cake. Use a scriber or headed pin to mark the side line-work, reflecting that of the board collar. Pipe graduated lines as before with two tiny dots in the apex of each curve.

Using a template made from the basic letter-ing (see page 15), add the baby's name. Arrange flowers around the base of the cake.

To remove the top collar from the waxed paper or plastic wrap, cover with a large piece of foam and then a thin cake board. Carefully turn it all over and remove the top board, exposing the paper or wrap, which should then be carefully peeled off.

Pipe a line of icing around the edge of the cake. Supporting the collar on both sides, turn over carefully and lift on to the cake, lining up the points with those on the board collar.

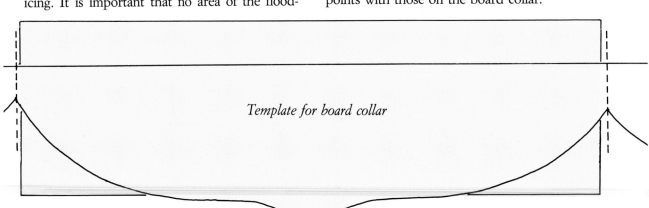

Template for board collar

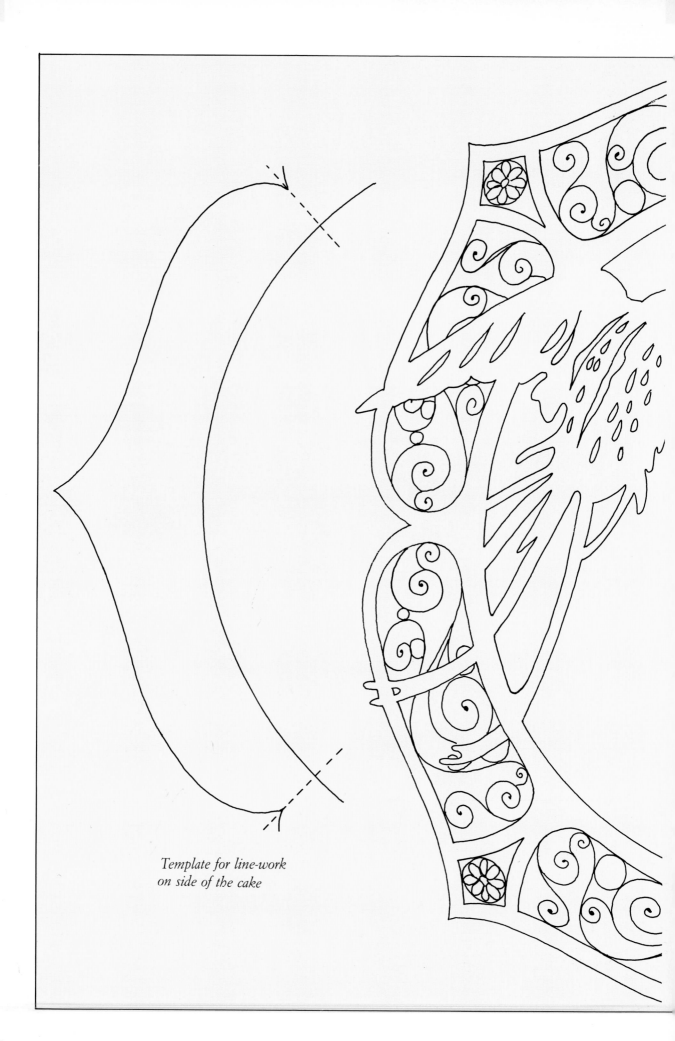

*Template for line-work
on side of the cake*

Template for top collar
NOTE: Check diameter of
finished cake before making
collar to ensure it will fit.

□ *DAISY* □

Ingredients

fruit cake baked in 20-cm (8-in) round cake tin (pan)
boiled, sieved apricot jam
700g (1½lb) marzipan
sherry or other alcohol
700g (1½lb) sugarpaste
burgundy, cornflower blue and lemon paste colourings (for flowers)
plum blossom tint

Equipment

27.5-cm (11-in) round cake board
pastry brush
rolling pin
tracing paper
scriber or headed pin
knitting needle
ribbon insert cutter
Garrett circular frill cutter
cocktail stick (wooden toothpick)
vegetable parchment piping bag
No0 nozzle
moulded daisies
moulded forget-me-nots
2.5 metres (2¾ yards) pink satin ribbon, 1.5-mm (¹⁄₁₆-in) wide
1 metre (1 yard) white lace ribbon, 12-mm (½-in) wide

A daisy chain encircles the baby on the top of this cake, which gives the illusion of having a frilled drape embroidered with broderie anglaise.

Cover the cake with marzipan and sugarpaste in the usual way. Coat the board and place the cake on it.

Measure the circumference of the cake and cut a strip of paper of the same length. Fold the paper into sixteen sections and cut a shallow scallop at the required height in the top edge. Wrap the paper around the cake and mark the scallops with a scriber or headed pin.

Mark a 15-cm (6-in) diameter circle on the top of the cake with a scriber.

Make a template of the broderie anglaise and lay this on the cake. Prick out the pattern with a scriber or headed pin, making sure that the centre flower of each group is set in the middle of a scallop and repeated in alternate scallops around the cake. Complete the broderie anglaise design (see page 11).

Using a ribbon insert cutter, make slits below the scallop guideline for the ribbons. Insert the 1.5-mm (¹⁄₁₆-in) pink ribbon (see page 14). This must be done before the frill is added.

Pipe a decorative border around the base of the cake and attach 1.5-mm (¹⁄₁₆-in) wide pink satin ribbon immediately above.

Make a very narrow frill using a circular frill cutter and attach to the marked guidelines by moistening with water.

Make a template of the baby and complete using the figure piping technique (see page 13). Leave to dry, then place on top of the cake.

Using a template made from the basic lettering (see page 15), add the baby's name.

Stick very small pieces of sugarpaste at intervals around the marked circle on the top of the cake. Instead of inserting the flower wires into the cake, cut these off short and press small groups of the daisies and forget-me-nots into the sugarpaste to form a circle.

Attach the lace ribbon to the edge of the cake board. Tie a double bow of the 1.5-mm (¹⁄₁₆-in) pink ribbon with trailing ends at the front of the cake.

Template for baby

Template for broderie anglaise

☐ *JASMINE* ☐

Ingredients

fruit cake baked in 20-cm (8-in) oval cake tin (pan)
boiled, sieved apricot jam
700g (1½lb) marzipan
sherry or other alcohol
700g (1½lb) sugarpaste
flower modelling paste
gum arabic glaze
brown liquid food colouring
black paste colouring
burgundy paste colouring
chestnut paste colouring
Christmas red paste colouring
egg yellow paste colouring
paprika paste colouring
black blossom tint
brown blossom tint

Equipment

27.5-cm (11-in) oval cake board
pastry brush
rolling pin
Garrett circular frill cutter
vegetable parchment piping bags
No0 nozzle
cocktail stick (wooden toothpick)
tracing paper
scriber or headed pin
very fine sable paintbrush
tweezers
28-gauge covered wire
small calyx cutter
leaf cutters
1 metre (1 yard) brown satin ribbon, 6-mm (¼-in)
  wide
Dresden modelling tool
dogbone modelling tool

This design is particularly suitable for an autumn christening with its theme of a babe in the wood.

Cover the cake with marzipan and place on the cake board. Cover the cake and the board with cream-coloured sugarpaste.

Using a circular frill cutter, make a double flounce (see page 14) and arrange around the base of the cake. This represents fungi and should be shaded when dry to make it more realistic.

Pipe a trail of ivy leaves by cutting a V-shape in the end of a piping bag, to conceal the join where the flounce was attached.

Make a template of the tree and the elf and lay on top of the cake. Prick out the design using a scriber and pipe directly on to the cake.

Place the baby on a bed of leaves made of sugarpaste in various shades of green and brown.

Blackberries

1 Roll a pea-sized ball of flower modelling paste to form the base and attach to a piece of hooked wire.
2 Make very small balls of dark red-coloured paste and stick to the base with egg white, starting underneath.
3 Cover the whole of the base with these small balls. If the balls or the base become too dry, they have a tendency to part company. Gum arabic glaze is a quite efficient way of solving this problem.
4 Cut a calyx with a small star calyx in green-coloured paste mixed with a little brown. Make a few cuts in each point of the calyx. Add a little egg white to the centre and slide on to the base of the blackberry.

Acorns

1 Make a ball of greenish-brown-coloured paste. Narrow it slightly to make an oval-shaped nut. Attach to a piece of hooked wire.
2 Form another piece of paste into a teardrop shape.
3 Hollow out with a modelling tool to make the cup.
4 Brush egg white into the cup and insert the wired nut. Mould the cup around the nut.
5 Push a brown stamen in the end for the dry flowerhead. Make ridges in the cup with tweezers.
6 Paint the nuts with gum arabic glaze and arrange in pairs surrounded with leaves.

Make some acorns and blackberries. Pipe the leaves directly on to the cake using the brush embroidery technique (see page 12).

Assemble the decorative material and arrange on the cake.

Using a template made from the basic lettering (see page 15), add the baby's name.

Moulded baby

If you do not wish to spend a lot of time modelling, a good alternative is to make a mould by pressing a small doll's face into modelling clay, either the self-drying type or the one that dries in a domestic oven. When the mould is ready, press a ball of flesh-coloured sugarpaste into the mould and re-shape the back of the head.

Roll a larger piece of sugarpaste into a ball, then roll into a pear shape for the body. Mark the prominent features of the thighs and buttocks. Shape a small cigar-shaped piece of sugar-paste for the arm and model a tiny hand.

Flatten the pointed end of the body while still soft and stick the head in position with icing. Then attach the arm. Paint in the hair and features.

To make the ear, flatten a tiny ball of paste between your thumb and finger, moisten and stick to the head. Model the contours with a pointed tool.

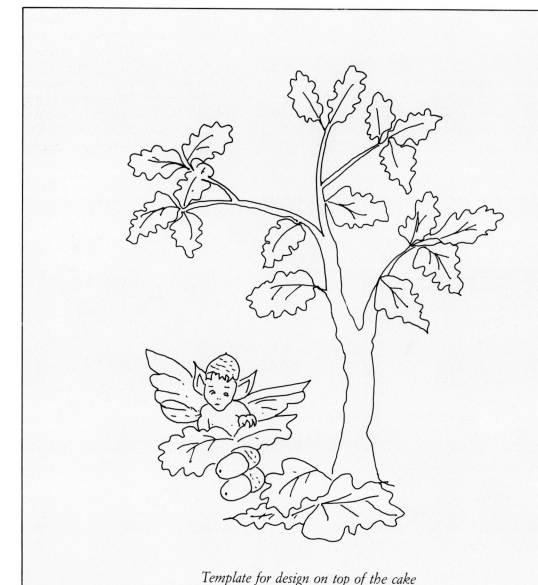

Template for design on top of the cake

□ POLLY AND ROBIN □

Ingredients
fruit cake baked in 20-cm (8-in) square cake tin
  (pan)
boiled, sieved apricot jam
700g (1½lb) marzipan
sherry or other alcohol
700g (1½lb) royal icing

Equipment
30-cm (12-in) square cake board
pastry brush
rolling pin
tracing paper
waxed paper or plastic wrap
vegetable parchment piping bags
No0 nozzle
No1 nozzle
No2 nozzle
No3 nozzle
scriber or headed pin
two 2.5-cm (1-in) high wooden or cork blocks
cocktail sticks (wooden toothpicks)

Parents of twin babies may wish to have a double christening cake, rather than separate cakes for each child.

Cover the cake with marzipan. Place on the board and coat with white royal icing in the usual way. When dry, coat the board with white royal icing.

Make a template of the collar and lay on a rigid surface. Cover with waxed paper or plastic wrap, carefully smoothing out any wrinkles. Using a No0 nozzle, pipe the filigree first, taking care that each line is securely attached to another. Then, using a No0 nozzle, pipe the collar outlines and flood these with soft icing (see page 13). Leave to dry.

Mark two lines on the top of the cake with a scriber as a guide for positioning the collars by laying the collar template flat on the cake and pricking along the straight side, making sure that the other side is right on the edge of the cake. Repeat this step on the opposite side of the cake. This will leave a strip about 4-cm (1½-in) wide across the centre of the cake where the babies' names may be added.

Make templates of the shapes 1 and 2 and use to mark guidelines for the embroidery on the sides of the cake. Pipe the embroidery using a No0 nozzle.

With a No2 nozzle pipe a row of beading around the base of the cake.

Make a template for the board line-work and lay it over each side of the cake board in turn,

with the straight edge touching the cake. Mark the outline with a scriber. Pipe over the guidelines with a No3 nozzle. Overpipe and pipe a line at the side using a No2 nozzle. Then overpipe all the lines using a No1 nozzle and pipe another line beside the other lines.

Attach the collars to the marked lines on the top of the cake with a little royal icing, propping each collar at the outside edge with two small blocks.

Pipe lines of extension work using a No0 nozzle from the collar to the cake. In the curved area, however, it will be easier to draw the threads of icing up from the cake to the collar. When the icing is dry, remove one block at a time and fill in the gap. Dry for 24 hours. Cover the join of the collar by piping neat embroidery. Pipe small dots on the edge of the collars.

Using a template made from the basic lettering (see page 15), add the babies' names.

Make a template of the stork and use to make two double-sided storks by figure piping (see page 13). Make a small hole in the icing of the cake and insert the storks attached to cocktail sticks (wooden toothpicks). Arrange crescents of flowers around the storks.

1 Lay a cocktail stick (wooden toothpick) on waxed paper and figure-pipe a stork over one end;
2 Pipe half-way down the stick to form the stork's straight leg and add the knotted bundle – leave to dry; 3 Turn the stork over and pipe the reverse side in the same way

Template for collar

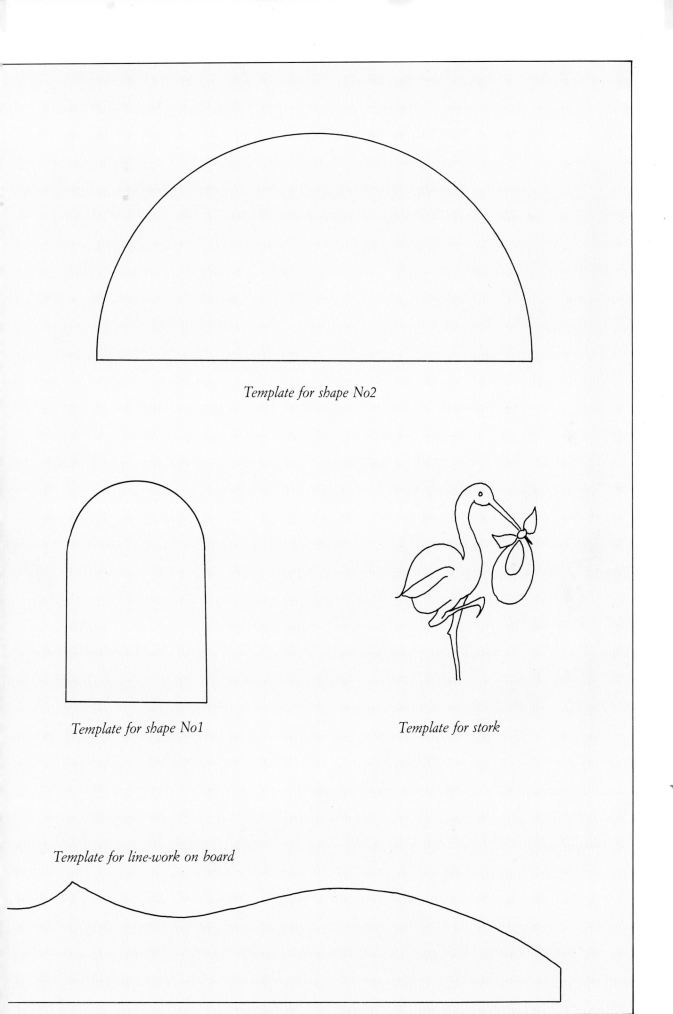

Template for shape No2

Template for shape No1

Template for stork

Template for line-work on board

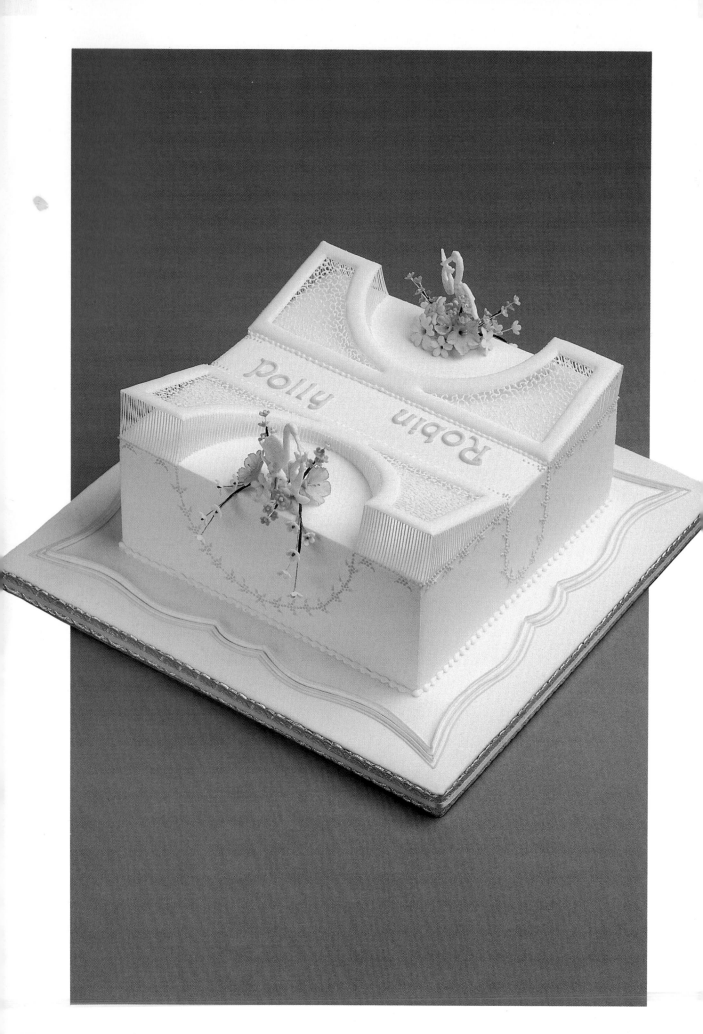